# HOW TO BE A PERSON

## CATHERINE NEWMAN

Storey Publishing

The mission of Storey Publishing is to serve our customers by
publishing practical information that encourages
personal independence in harmony with the environment.

**Edited by Deanna F. Cook and Michal Lumsden**
**Art direction and book design by Alethea Morrison**
**Text production by Kristy MacWilliams**
**Illustrations by © Debbie Fong**
**Text © 2020 by Catherine Newman**

**Storey books are available at special discounts when purchased in bulk for
premiums and sales promotions as well as for fund-raising or educational use.
Special editions or book excerpts can also be created to specification. For
details, please call 800-827-8673, or send an email to sales@storey.com.**

**Storey Publishing**
**210 MASS MoCA Way**
**North Adams, MA 01247**
**storey.com**

Printed in the United States by Versa Press
10  9  8  7  6  5  4  3

Library of Congress Cataloging-in-Publication Data

Names: Newman, Catherine, 1968- author.
Title: How to be a person / Catherine Newman.
Description: North Adams : Storey Publishing, 2020. | Audience: Ages 10–14 | Audience:
Grades 4–6 | Summary: "Catherine Newman has written the ultimate guidebook for kids,
jam-packed with tips, tricks, and skills to become a more dependable person"— Provided by
publisher.
Identifiers: LCCN 2019056617 (print) | LCCN 2019056618 (ebook) | ISBN 9781635861822
(paperback) | ISBN 9781635861839 (ebook)
Subjects: LCSH: Self-presentation—Juvenile literature. | Self-actualization (Psychology)—
Juvenile literature.
Classification: LCC BF697.5.S44 N489 2020  (print) | LCC BF697.5.S44 (ebook) | DDC
155.42/491—dc23
LC record available at https://lccn.loc.gov/2019056617
LC ebook record available at https://lccn.loc.gov/2019056618

For Ben and Birdy and everyone else who's
trying to be their best selves — all of us.
We got this.
— Catherine


For Allistair, Murray, and Cooper.
— Debbie

# CONTENTS

# BECOMING YOUR BEST SELF

We swear we're not trying to turn you into a premature adult! We don't want you trudging around in a small suit with a briefcase or wedging yourself under the sink to fix the plumbing in your bathroom. But we do think you'll be a happier person if you learn the skills in this book — some of which you probably already know, others of which people probably think you already know (*shhhh*), and all of which will come in handy pretty much immediately. The truth is that it feels good to do meaningful things, and it feels good to be appreciated, and these skills pretty much guarantee a combination of those two good feelings.

Look, we understand that maybe you didn't pick this book out all on your own. Maybe your grown-ups even passive-aggressively gave it to you for your birthday along with a pair of rubber gloves and a plunger. (You're welcome!) But it doesn't really matter, because we're convinced that a lot of the tasks we tend to think of as *chores* can be truly rewarding — especially if you have a chance to step toward them with confidence rather than being backed into them by that bulldozer of nagging otherwise known as your mom or dad. Or maybe by the time you're reading this, there's a robot that can do all of the household chores! Perfect. Put this book aside to show your children one day. "Before we had robots, we had to water the plants and wipe the kitchen counters ourselves!" you'll say, and the kids will shake their heads and pity you.

One thing we know: asking, "What can I do to help?" is a sure way to be your best self. And with this book in hand, you won't have to say awkwardly, "Um, I don't actually know how to do that!"

**A note:** if you have different abilities — neurologically, cognitively, or physically — then some of these skills might require various kinds of adaptation and hacking. We'd love to hear your thoughts about how to make this book work better for you: choose "contact" from the menu on my website, catherinenewmanwriter.com.

*Catherine*

# OTHER BEINGS

## How to Care for the People, Pets, and Plants in Your Life

-- -- -- -- -- -- -- -- -- -- -- -- -- -- -- --

Someone can feel looked after by you without you doing anything at all. You could be just smiling or sitting nearby. But some situations require more active caretaking, and these are a handful of them.

# HOW TO
# CHEER UP SICK PEOPLE

If someone in your house is sick, you can bring them something soothing, like a glass of ginger ale, a bowl of soup, or some scrambled eggs on toast. Or keep them company while they watch TV or do a puzzle book or look through the box of old holiday cards.

If a friend is sick, you could drop by* with flowers or a magazine, or send a card.

For a classmate who's been sick for a while, you could gather cards from the whole class and send them in a big envelope.

* Wash your hands when you leave if it's something you could catch!

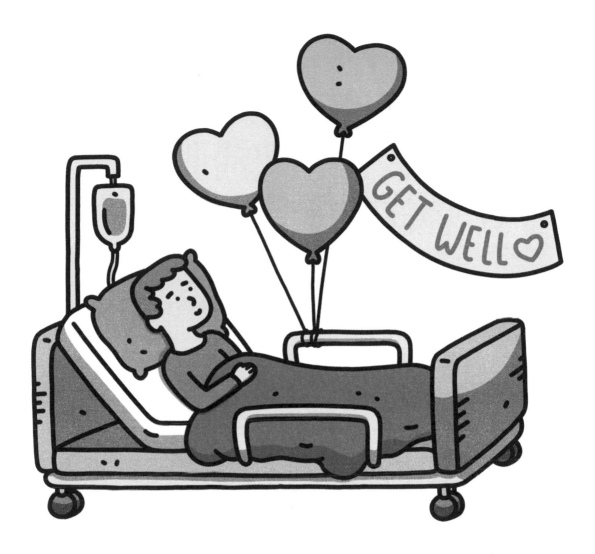

## Bring some sunshine.

It's nice to visit someone who's in the hospital and bring a homemade card or even a "Get Well" banner to hang by their bed. You might need to gather your courage, because hospitals can be a little frightening, but you don't need to stay long, and your sick person will be so happy to see your face! They're still the same person under there, even if they are surrounded by weird tubes and blankets or a hospital-y smell.

# HOW TO BRING A LITTLE SUNSHINE TO OLDER FOLKS

Just the fact of you being there is likely to bring cheer! But you could offer to play a game (they might want to teach you a strange one you've never heard of) or do a jigsaw puzzle or read to them, if that's something they might like.

HOWZABOUT A QUICK GAME OF SNIP-SNAP-SNOREM?

If you are good with nail polish, your person might say yes to a manicure!

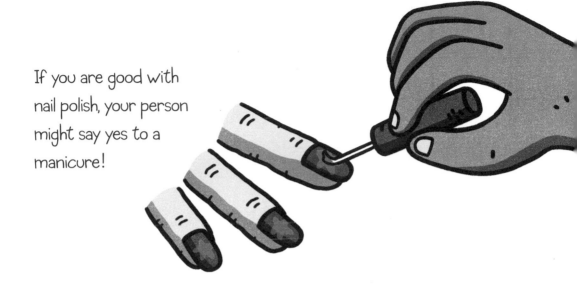

If you play an instrument, sing, tell jokes, or do magic tricks, your older person will likely be a very appreciative audience, and you will end up feeling like a STAR.

# HOW TO
# BE WITH A BABY OR A LITTLE KID

Maybe you've got teeny-tiny guests at home — or even a whole new sibling. Whatever the reason, there's a baby in the house, so you will want to pay attention to it!

* Be patient and gentle. Babies might need a little time to get to know you!

* Ask an adult to help you learn how to hold the baby safely, what the baby likes, and if there are any books or toys for the baby. If you'd like to help feed or bathe the baby, just ask!

* Don't freak out if the baby, uh, gets something on you. Babies are messy, and they can't help it.

* Play with the baby or toddler the way they like. Maybe the baby wants you to build the tallest block tower ever, but then just wants to knock the blocks down — over and over and over again. Or they might want you to "read" the same board book with no words in it over and over and over again. Okay!

* Ask an adult if there's anything dangerous you should worry about, such as choking hazards, electrical outlets, or food allergies.

* Ask for help if you need it.

If you're interested in **babysitting**, consider working first as a **parent's helper** — which means watching a baby or child while a parent or other caregiver is in another part of the house, but still available to step in and help if you need them.

# HOW TO
# HELP SOMEONE
## (INCLUDING YOURSELF)
# FALL ASLEEP

Lots of people — including little kids, big kids, older folks, and fretful folks — have a hard time falling asleep. There are many strategies to try. Feel free to mix and match as much as you like!

### A sleepy mugful.

Warm milk actually contains a neurochemical called tryptophan, and although the science isn't clear on whether or not this actually helps you fall asleep, creating an association between sleep and a comforting mug of warm, nourishing milk definitely can.

Chamomile tea may also scientifically help or psychologically help. Either way it's good.

## Aromatherapy.

Chamomile and lavender essential oils are thought to be relaxing. You can shake a few drops into a hot bath, onto a tissue near your pillow, or into a diffuser, which is like a tiny humidifier.

## Relaxation techniques.

Try a little yoga or stretching, or meditate for 2 to 5 minutes. (There are apps for this.) Put on some relaxing music, preferably without distracting lyrics.

## Pure sleep space.

Avoid reading or working in bed and keep cell phones out of your bedroom. You want to create an association between bed and sleep.

**The placebo effect** is a really powerful tool! Just because something is "all in your head" doesn't mean it's not real. So if you tell yourself that whatever you're doing is going to help you fall asleep, it will.

# HOW TO
# TAKE CARE OF A PET

Okay, we can't really teach you how exactly to care for your gecko or cockatiel or cocker spaniel, but there are some basic ways to approach caring for a pet that are helpful.

**FEED ME CRICKETS!**

**FEED ME SEEDS!**

**FEED ME STEAK!**

✳ Love them. That's easy — you and your pet will both get so much out of the relationship.

✳ Remind yourself that animals are dependent on us to take care of them. It's kind of a huge responsibility, and we honor it by remembering to give them what they need.

✳ If it's your job to give your lizard fresh water or take the dog for an afternoon walk, you can make a schedule for yourself or create a visual reminder. (Lots of animals will find ways to remind you, but some can't.)

✳ If you are responsible for a particular chore — scooping the cat litter or changing the hamster's bedding, say — be sure to do it, even if it's gross.

✳ When you have a couple of extra minutes in your day, brush your pet or play with them. They'll love that!

LITTER BOX

THANK YOU!

# HOW TO CARE FOR HOUSEPLANTS

Houseplants ask for so little and give us so much! Green leaves to look at, more oxygen to breathe, and even (sometimes) flowers or fruit.

plants

sunny window sill

watering can

tray to protect your window sill

All plants ask for is some sunlight and not to be over- or underwatered. That's right. They want to be watered just the right amount.

**Fun Fact.** People are more likely to water plants too much than too little!

If your plant came with a tag saying what it likes, great! You'll know how much water and sunlight it needs, and you can put it in a sunny window sill (or not, if it prefers shade) and create a little watering schedule for yourself.

If your plant didn't come with a tag, then stick your finger up to its first knuckle into the soil. If you can feel dampness, it probably doesn't need water yet.

If it's dry, then add water until it drips out of the drainage holes at the bottom of the pot — which means that it has had enough.

You can also look up your plant online or in a book to learn more about what it needs.

If your plant starts to seem unhappy, you can try giving it a little bit of plant fertilizer. Or move it into a bigger pot so it can spread out a little.

Cacti look like little cartoon plants and are easy to take care of. Mostly they just like to be in a warm sunny spot where you can ignore them — aside from telling them how cute they are and watering them every now and then.

# HOW TO BE A WELCOME GUEST

Yay! You got invited to a friend's house. If there's one message you want to communicate to your host, it's "I'm so happy to be here!"

If you run into other family members in the house, introduce yourself.

If you're not sure about something, just ask.

If your host offers you choices about what to do, go ahead and pick something. (Saying, "I don't care" is not usually that helpful.)

Assuming it's okay with your grown-ups, follow the house rules when you're at someone else's place. This might mean something more fun than at your house (they drink soda with dinner and you only drink milk) or something less fun (kids do the dinner dishes and they don't have a dishwasher). Whatever it is, just go with the flow.

When it's time to leave, try to find your friend's family to thank them and say goodbye.

THANK YOU SO MUCH FOR HAVING ME OVER! I HAD A REALLY NICE TIME.

# POP QUIZ!

You're eating dinner at a friend's house and you knock your cup over, spilling milk all over the place. You:

**A** Scream and run out of the room and out of the house and all the way home, screaming.

**B** Laugh milk out of your nose while their dog laps up the puddles.

**C** Wait for the robot maid to roll in and clean it up.

**D** Say, "I'm so sorry! Is there a dish towel I can use to clean this up?"

**Answer:** D, of course. And maybe B, but only in addition to — not instead of — D.

# HOW TO
# BE A GRACIOUS HOST

Yay! You've got a friend over. If there's one message you want to communicate to your guest, it's "I'm so glad you're here!"

Introduce them to your family.

Offer your guest a snack and something to drink.

Let your guest choose how to spend the time together, and give them some choices — listening to music, playing a game, going for a tour of the neighborhood — if they're not sure what to do.

Show your guest to the door when it's time to say goodbye.

Stash your phones, unless you're using them to do something together.

# HOW TO
# WRAP A PRESENT

You got invited to a party! Or maybe it's a holiday. Anyway, you've got a present to give. And even if you're giving the smallest gift, wrapping it makes it all the more special.

Even a painted rock deserves a nice wrapping job!

**Bag it.** The easiest way is to wrap a gift loosely in tissue paper and put it in a gift bag. (This is especially good for odd-shaped things.) Stuff some more crumpled tissue paper on top to hide the gift and make the bag look festive.

**Or box it up.** Put the gift in a box and then wrap the box (like we show on the next page). You'll need wrapping paper, scissors, clear tape, and ribbon or twine for this method. Oh, and a hard surface (not the couch or a carpet). This is the same way you'd wrap something that starts out rectangular, like a book or a game.

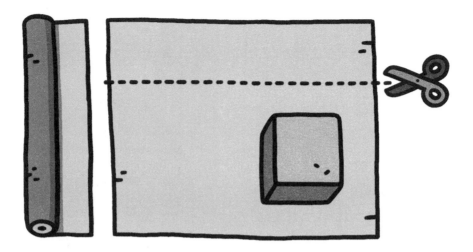

**1** Cut a big enough* piece of paper to go around the box (or book or whatever you're wrapping). You'll want the paper long enough so that it goes all the way around the box and wide enough so that there's extra to cover the side of the box.

\* Do you know the expression "measure twice, cut once"? So, yeah.

**2** Wrap the paper around the box, pull it tight, and press a piece of tape along the seam where the paper meets itself.

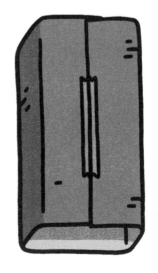

**3** Finish one side at a time: With the seam still facing up, fold down the top flap onto one side of the box, making two little wings at the side. Flatten the wings in against the box, then fold the remaining paper up against the box. Press a piece of tape to the seam where the paper meets itself.

Repeat with the other side of the box. It doesn't need to be perfect.

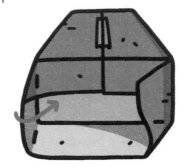

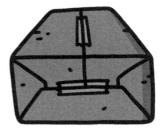

## ADD RIBBON!

**1** Keep the ribbon (or twine) still attached to the spool and wrap it loosely around the box three times to measure. Cut it.

**2** With the seam still facing up, slide the ribbon under the box and stretch the ends over the box, lining them up and pulling them tight.

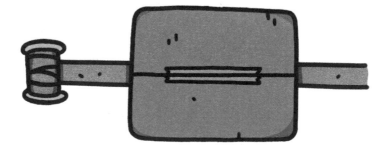

**3** Cross the ribbon and pull the ends toward the other sides of the box.

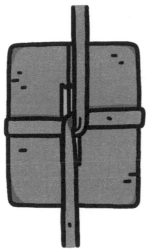

**4** Flip the box over and tie a bow on top! You will need someone else to press a finger on the ribbon to hold it tight as you're tying it. (Or you can try growing a third arm!) Trim the excess ribbon.

# SAYING IT RIGHT

## How to Be Kind and Get Your Point Across

- - - - - - - - - - - - - - - - - - - - - - - -

Communicating clearly and well is an important part of being a person, caring for other people, changing the world, and (to be honest) getting what you want. Here are some basic tools to help you do all those things.

# HOW TO WRITE A THANK-YOU NOTE

Someone gave you something or did something nice on your behalf! Lucky you! Now you get to thank them. And even though you already thanked your friend at the party for the origami paper, or texted a quick "Thanks for the $, Grandma!!!!" it is so nice to send (and receive) a handwritten thank-you note. And it honestly takes, like, 1 minute to do it. You totally have 1 minute!

Of course there's no single formula! But here's a, uh, single formula. Just adapt it however you need to, and make sure to add just a sentence or two more than "Thank you for the _____."

**1** Dear _____,

**2** Thank you so much for the _____.

**3** I can't wait to spend it on _____ [or] play with/wear/ do _____ with it.

**4** It's exactly my favorite color/style/kind of _____. You know me so well!

 I'm so glad you were at my party [or] I hope I get to see you soon.

 Love, _____

If someone did something nice for you rather than giving you a gift, just thank them for whatever it was they did, being sure to add something about how helpful it was.

DEAR MRS. MOONWALKER,

IT WAS SO KIND OF YOU TO DONATE THAT HOMEMADE GRANOLA TO OUR BOY SCOUTS FUNDRAISER! I'M SURE WHOEVER WON IT WAS REALLY EXCITED TO EAT IT FOR BREAKFAST THE NEXT DAY. THANK YOU SO MUCH FOR YOUR GENEROSITY.

YOURS TRULY,
JACK

# POP QUIZ!

Your aunt knit you a terrible sweater for your birthday! It's itchy and ugly and it has buttons (you hate buttons), but at least it's your favorite color. What should you include in your thank-you note?

**A** It is amazing to me that you could manage to create a sweater that is both ugly *and* uncomfortable!

**B** You sure as heck knit a sweater! Thanks for it.

**C** Dear Auntie, Thank you for the present. Love, me

**D** Dear Auntie, Remember when you taught me to knit? It took me six months to make that one lopsided pot holder! I can't believe you knit me a whole entire sweater. And you picked out yarn that is, as you know, my absolute favorite color in the world! Thank you for being the best aunt ever. I am so lucky to be your nephew. xoxo

**Answer:** D, of course. It is always possible to be truthful in a thank-you note — to feel and express gratitude for the act of someone caring enough to do or buy something for you — even if you didn't get your favorite-ever present.

# HOW TO WRITE A CONDOLENCE* NOTE

If someone close to you loses someone close to them — their grandma, their old beagle, a beloved anybody — then it's nice to write a condolence note. The point is just to say, "I'm sorry" — not in the sense of "I apologize," but in the sense of, "I wish you didn't have to feel this grief." A condolence note can be short. You're just reminding the person that their community is there to support them while they're sad.

*Condolence means "an expression of sympathy."

DEAR ANGELA,

I WAS SO SORRY TO HEAR ABOUT BUFFY THE VAMPIRE SLAYER. SHE WAS SUCH A GREAT CAT, AND I ALWAYS LOVED IT WHEN SHE CAME AND SAT IN THE BOX WHILE WE PLAYED MONOPOLY. YOU MUST MISS HER SO MUCH. I'M THINKING OF YOU.

LOVE,

SAM

# HOW TO ADDRESS AN ENVELOPE

## RIGHT

your name and address in the upper left corner (or on the back flap)

full name of the person you're mailing it to

postage stamp in the upper right corner

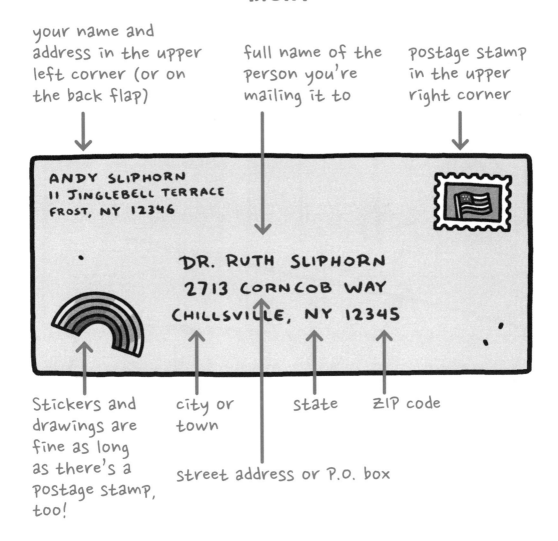

ANDY SLIPHORN
11 JINGLEBELL TERRACE
FROST, NY 12346

DR. RUTH SLIPHORN
2713 CORNCOB WAY
CHILLSVILLE, NY 12345

Stickers and drawings are fine as long as there's a postage stamp, too!

city or town

state

ZIP code

street address or P.O. box

> **Fun Fact.** The truth is, the post office is pretty forgiving, and your letter is likely to get there even if you don't follow the rules exactly. You could even put an address label on a potato and, as long as you put enough postage on it, the post office will deliver it.

## WRONG

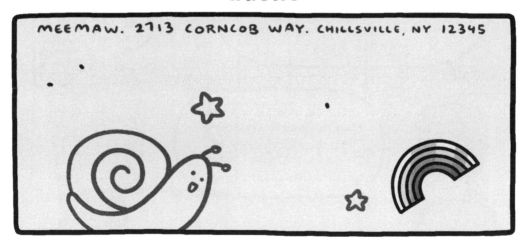

MEEMAW. 2713 CORNCOB WAY. CHILLSVILLE, NY 12345

(Though if you put a stamp on it, it would probably get to your Meemaw anyway.)

If you're sending mail to a different country, the address might look different. Make sure to include the country name and find out what kind of stamp you need.

# HOW TO
# APOLOGIZE

If something you did hurt somebody else, take responsibility for it and apologize, even if you didn't mean to do it or say it or cause any harm. Imagining the other person's feelings is called empathy, and it's super-helpful to experience and to express.

# HOW TO
# INCLUDE SOMEONE

People end up alone for lots of reasons: they're new; they're different from most of the people at your school; other people think they're weird. Those are all good reasons to reach out. This might mean: inviting them to sit with you and your friends; saying, "Can I join you?" and plunking down your lunch tray; including them in a get-together; or simply smiling when you pass in the hallway. You — yes, you — can make all the difference in the world. And one day, when you're new or lonely yourself, you'll be so glad when someone else reaches out.

**Fun Fact.** Lots of "weird" people turn out to be really cool. (But you already know that.)

# HOW TO HAVE A CONVERSATION

If you ever feel awkward talking to somebody, just ask a question. That gives them an opportunity to talk—and it gives you an opportunity to learn more about them. That's a great recipe for conversation!

When the other person is speaking, you can show that you're listening by making eye contact, nodding, asking follow-up questions, and saying back what you hear them say.

## YOUR QUESTIONS CAN BE

### Deep

WHERE DO YOU THINK YOU ARE BEFORE YOU ARE BORN?

### Goofy

WOULD YOU RATHER BE A HEDGEHOG OR A RAINCLOUD?

## GOOD LISTENING

...ALTHOUGH IT WOULD BE NICE TO LIVE IN A BURROW WITH THE OTHER HEDGEHOGS...

PLUS, IF YOU WERE A HEDGEHOG, THEN YOU WOULDN'T HAVE TO RAIN ON EVERYBODY WHICH YOU SAID YOU'D HATE!

## BAD LISTENING

...BUT THEN I GUESS I WOULDN'T REALLY WANT TO BE SO PRICKLY...

MM HM.

**Fun Fact.** A study found that people tend to assume their conversation partners enjoy their company less than they actually do. In other words, you're more fun to be around than you think! It doesn't matter if you're weird or awkward. Just be yourself.

# HOW TO
# ASK FOR SOMETHING
# OVER E-MAIL

You'll need to ask for a lot of favors in your life! You'll want teachers to write you recommendation letters, managers to switch your shift at Cinnabon, grandparents to donate to your Bagpipe Club fundraiser. The key to asking for something over e-mail is to be clear about what you're asking, to be polite, and to express your gratitude.

## WRONG

| To: | Jeremy Snodgrass |
|---|---|
| Subject: | chemistry, which sux |

Hey Snotgrass, my paper's late. Sorry, dude! k

# RIGHT

To: Jeremy Snodgrass

Subject: Request for an extension ①

Dear Mr. Snodgrass, ②

I'm writing to ask for a two-day extension on the
Chemistry research paper due next Wednesday. ③
I finally have a handle on my topic (You're Not So
Basic: The pH Scale of People) which I'm excited
about, but I was struggling for a few days, and it
set me back. I'd be so grateful if you'd let me turn
it in on Friday. ④

Yours truly, ⑤
Kevin

---

① The subject line is clear
and direct.

② There's a friendly greeting
and a proper form of address,
such as Ms., Dr., or Mr.

③ You're giving the person a
reasonable amount of time
to deal with whatever
you're asking.

④ You express your appreciation
for the person's assistance.

⑤ There's a polite sign-off.

If they agree to whatever
you're asking, then don't
forget to thank them (see
page 34).

# HOW TO
# FILL OUT A FORM

You're going to fill out a lot of forms in your life — starting, well, now. Library card requests, doctor's office questionnaires, job applications, online orders, school and sports permission forms, learner's permit and driver's license applications . . . so many forms. If you've ever done Mad Libs, then you totally know how to fill out a form! (Just don't put in words like "fried egg" and "poopy.") Here's how:

**Read through the whole form first** and check for instructions such as whether to "print" (this means clear, separate letters as opposed to cursive), use pen or pencil in a specific ink color, or get a signature from a parent or guardian.

**Fill in your name.** You might write it all on one line, or it might be last name then first name, or you might need to fit each letter in a little box.

**There might be dates to fill out** — like today's or your birthday. The format (MM/DD/YYYY) means that you should fill in the month as two numbers, then the date, then the year. October 6, 2030, would be 10/06/2030.

**You might need to sign the form** if it asks for a signature. That means writing your whole name out in your own way, in cursive if you know how (see example). ⟶

# Practice on a magazine subscription card —

the kind that falls out when you open the magazine.

SUBSCRIBE

1 YEAR $12

Heywood Yapinchme
NAME

111 Pickle Parkway
ADDRESS

Slickpoo, ID 83555
CITY / STATE / ZIP

pinchme@slickpoo.gov
EMAIL ADDRESS

☐ PAYMENT ENCLOSED
☐ BILL ME LATER

*Heywood Yapinchme*

Practice Signature

# HOW TO
# ANSWER
# THE PHONE

If your phone rings — either a cell phone or landline — tap the green button or the word "answer" (cell) or lift up the receiver (landline) and say, "Hello." (When someone calls you, you need to be the one to speak first).

RIIIIING!

Talking on the phone is easiest if you are quiet and attentive — that is, not chewing, whistling, playing the ukulele, or paying close attention to something else, like TV, your gerbil Eeny-Beeny, or algebra.

If you don't recognize the caller's number or voice, say, "May I ask who's calling?"

# HOW TO MAKE A PHONE CALL

When you call someone else, the phone will ring and then they will speak first, usually by saying, "Hello." Identify yourself and explain why you're calling.

If your call goes to voice mail, there will be something like a beep or a tone cuing you to leave a clear, brief message, including your name, your phone number, and what you're hoping will happen next.

**RIGHT**

HI! MY NAME IS ELLEN ROAN AND I'M CALLING TO SEE IF YOU HAVE THE GAME "JOCKEYING EQUESTRIANS" AT YOUR STORE. MY NUMBER IS 123-123-1234. PLEASE LET ME KNOW. THANK YOU.

**WRONG**

...AND I WAS LIKE, ARE YOU KIDDING ME?

A NEW HORSE-THEMED VIDEO GAME? I AM SO ALL OVER THAT...

Texting gives you plenty of time to figure out how you want to write or respond to someone else. Making a phone call is a little trickier because it involves a conversation happening here and now, and you can't start over as easily. But you can do it! Worst case scenario, you act kind of dorky, and that's fine.

# HOW TO CONTACT YOUR POLITICAL REPRESENTATIVES

If there's an issue you care about, then do something about it! Contact your political representatives — senators, House representatives, state or local politicians — and let them know how you feel. You can do this even if you're not old enough to vote!

**1 Do your research** to find out where the issue is playing out — whether it's in Congress, your state government, or right in your own town.

**2 Figure out who represents you.** If you type in your address at whoaremyrepresentatives.org, you'll get a list, from the current president to your state's governor to the elected officials of your city or town.

**3 Look them up** to find their contact information: there will likely be phone numbers, e-mail addresses, and mailing addresses.

**4** **Decide how you want to reach out.** A phone call can be a little nerve-wracking (see page 50), but it's quick. You will likely leave a voice-mail message or talk to an aide (a person who works for the politician), and you can keep it short and to the point. There may even be a script online that you can follow.

HI. MY NAME IS ALAN JUGGLER. I LIVE HERE IN IDAHO, AND I'M CALLING TO LET THE GOVERNOR KNOW THAT I'M REALLY WORRIED ABOUT THE POTATO MASHERS' STRIKE.* I'M HOPING SHE'LL SUPPORT THEIR DEMANDS FOR BETTER PAY.

If you prefer, you can send an e-mail or a snail-mail letter that says more or less the same thing.

*Not a real issue.

UNI THE
NO
DON'T MASH OUR WAGES!

.THIS IS WHAT DEMOCRACY LOOKS LIKE

FAIR AY

PAY
NO POTATOES

# DIRTY THINGS

## How to Clean and Care for Your Home

- - - - - - - - - - - - - - - - - - - -

It doesn't really matter how chores work in your home — whether they're assigned to you or your allowance depends on them, whether there's a chores wheel or everyone pitches in as the need arises. What matters is that you learn the basics of housework. (Then, if you don't do something, at least it's not because you don't know how!)

# HOW TO
# LOAD THE
# DISHWASHER

**1** Scrape the leftover food off the dishes into the trash or compost. To make sure your dishes get all-the-way clean, rinse them too. (This is especially important if your dishwasher was made during the Pleistocene Era.)

**2** Load large and heavy things, like dinner plates and casseroles, on the bottom rack. Give everything plenty of room. Plates fit in the slots and may need to lean a bit. Anything that can be filled (such as bowls or pots) should be loaded with the open side down so they don't fill with water.

**3** Arrange glasses, mugs, cooking utensils, and anything small, plastic, or delicate* in the top rack. Again, openings should face down so that you don't end up with cups full of icky dishwater.

*Some delicate or fancy or sharp things might not go in the dishwasher. Ask before loading.

**4** Load the silverware in the silverware basket, with the dirty part facing out or up. Arrange sharp knives blade down, so they don't stab anyone.

**Tip:** Load each type of silverware together to make unloading nice and easy.

**5** Look inside and make sure that nothing is sticking up into the place where something is going to be spinning around (e.g., the spray arm).

**6** Put detergent wherever it goes (ask if you're not sure) and choose the setting you need ("normal cycle" unless someone tells you otherwise), then hit "start" and you're done.

# HOW TO
# EMPTY THE
# DISHWASHER

**1** Grab a dry dish towel, in case anything is still a bit wet as you're unloading.

**2** Put dishes away on shelves or in cupboards, dealing with one type at a time to make it easier. If you don't know where something goes — especially stuff like storage containers or serving plates — just ask.

**3** Sort the silverware into the silverware drawer.

# POP QUIZ!

Your grown-ups ask you to deal with the dishes after dinner in the cabin. You can't help noticing that there is (cue horror-movie music) *no dishwasher!* You:

**A** Fling the dishes into the woods and hope nobody notices.

**B** Hide the dishes in the oven and hope nobody notices.

**C** Say "Oops!" really loud and drop them all on the floor, then sweep up the broken pieces (see page 66) and throw them away.

**D** Wash them by hand.

**Answer:** D. Don't panic! Turn the page to learn how you do it . . .

# HOW TO HAND-WASH DISHES

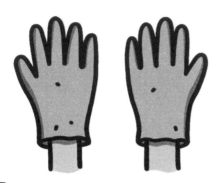

**1** Roll up your sleeves and put on some rubber gloves if you've got them.

**2** If there's a super-crusty pot or pan, fill it with hot water and a squirt of soap and leave it on the counter while you deal with the rest.

**3** Put a stopper in the sink, then fill the sink with hot water and add a few squirts of dish soap.

**4** Wash in order from cleanest to dirtiest: the glasses, dishes, and silverware, then the pots and pans and cooking utensils. Use a sponge and scrub everything so that there is no visible crud on it and so that it doesn't feel greasy between your fingers. Drain and refill the water if it gets really mucky.

**5** If it's a double sink, then fill the second basin with clean hot water, and dip the dishes in it to rinse the soap off of them. Otherwise fill a basin or your largest bowl with hot water for rinsing.

**6** Hand the rinsed dishes to someone who's standing around with a dish towel, or put them in a drying rack, angled so that water can drain out of them as they dry.

**7** Don't "forget" those crusty pots! Do them last, and use the scrubby side of the sponge or some other type of scrubber to get them clean.

**8** Drain the sink and wipe it out with a sponge. Shake the gross stuff out of the drain baskets into the trash. Squeeze the extra water out of the sponge and put it where it goes.

# HOW TO
# WIPE THE TABLE AND COUNTERS

If your job was clearing the table and/or doing the dishes, then the last step is wiping down the surfaces.

**1** Move things like salt shakers and candlesticks out of the way.

**2** Wipe up all the crumbs first by cupping your hand at the edge of the surface and sweeping the crumbs into it.

RIGHT                    WRONG*

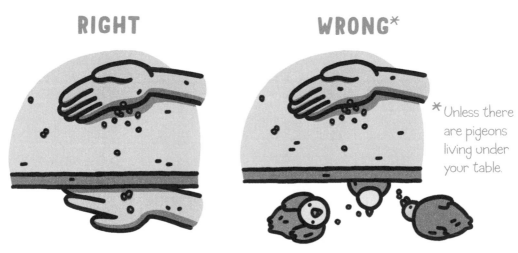

*Unless there are pigeons living under your table.

**3** Wet and then wring out a sponge so that it's damp but not sopping. Then wipe down the table.

**4** Tackle any sticky or greasy spots, using a splash of white vinegar or a spritz of cleaner if you need it. Then give the surface one final wipe with the freshly dampened sponge.

# HOW TO TAKE OUT THE TRASH

This is nobody's favorite chore! But someone has to do it — and if you notice that the trash stinks or is full, that someone should be you. If your family composts or recycles, then there will be added steps in your trash routine! (That sounds like a not-very-fun dance.)

1 Tie the bag closed. If there's a tie at the top of the bag, then pull the two sides to cinch up the top and tie them together. If not, check the box of bags and see if there are twist ties. Grab the neck of the

bag and twist it. Then wrap the tie around the neck and twist the tie's ends together tightly.

2 Bring the bag to the garbage can outside your house or the garbage chute in your building, or wherever the trash goes.

## POP QUIZ!

### You took out the trash. Now what?

**A** Pin a gold star to yourself.

**B** Clap your hands noisily and yell, "Mission accomplished! You're welcome."

**C** Put a new trash bag in the empty bin and knot or cinch it so that it doesn't slide down like a sock with no elastic in it.

**D** All of the above.

**Answer:** C or D. Feel free to engage in a long, trashy process of self-congratulation, as long as you remember the new bag.

# HOW TO SWEEP THE FLOOR

**1** Clear the floor of clutter like shoes and coats. (Why is your mom's coat on the floor anyway?)

**2** Shut your pets in a different room, even if they think they want to help.

**3** Hold the broom comfortably and sweep slowly in one direction at a time, from the corners of the room toward the center. Pull the broom so that it sweeps gently across the floor, creating piles as you sweep.

**4** Use a dustpan and broom (or a little hand broom, if you've got one) to sweep up the piles and escort them to the trash.

# POP QUIZ!

You've swept the pile of dust and dirt into the dustpan. It doesn't all go in the dustpan, though. In fact, the pile seems to leave behind a strip of dust and dirt that the dustpan kind of refuses to deal with. You:

**A** Keep at it. Eventually the dirt line will get so thin that it will technically kind of more or less not even be there anymore.

**B** Wipe it up with a damp paper towel or a loop of tape and then shine up your halo with a clean rag.

**C** Kind of flick it around with the broom on-purpose-by-accident so that it "disappears."

**D** Any or all of the above.

**Answer:** D. It's not you — it's the dustpan. Just do your best. We only want you to be a regular, clean-enough person. We're not trying to win you a prize as the World's Cleanest Person Ever.

# HOW TO
# VACUUM

The vacuum is noisy and scary and the mortal enemy of pets. Still, it's useful for cleaning the floor.

**1** **First pick up the floor.** No, don't pick up the floor. You know what we mean. Move the stray LEGOs and LEGO catalogues and slippers so you don't have to vacuum around them and so you won't suck them up by mistake.

I PROMISE I WON'T SHED ANYMORE!

**2** **Plug in the vacuum cleaner,** turn it on, and vacuum the edges and underneaths of the room using the hose and the brush attachments. If the vacuum is quiet and not working well, that means you forgot to turn it on.

**3** **Vacuum the middle** of the room by going back and forth and then back and forth the other way. Don't vacuum the vacuum's cord!

**4** **Turn off the vacuum cleaner,** unplug it, roll up the cord, and return it to its home — along with anything else you moved along the way.

**Extra credit.** Learn how to change the bag or empty the canister where the dirt goes. (This can be weirdly satisfying in a "Wow, I sure vacuumed up a lot of crud!" kind of way.)

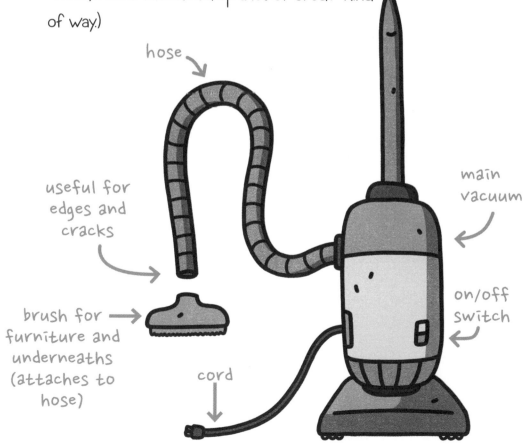

hose

useful for edges and cracks

brush for furniture and underneaths (attaches to hose)

cord

main vacuum

on/off switch

# HOW TO
# CLEAN A BATHROOM

Put on a pair of rubber gloves, grab the supplies your family uses, and then:

## CLEAN THE COUNTERS AND SINK

**1** Clear all the stuff off the counter.

Put the stuff from the counter in a bin or basket while you clean.

**2** Spritz the counters, sink, and faucet with vinegar or cleaning spray and wipe everything thoroughly with a sponge.

**3** Rinse the sponge and wipe everything down.

**4** If the sink is still dirty, you may need to sprinkle on baking soda or scrubby powder and rub it hard with the sponge.

**5** Put everything back on the counters.

# The Very Basic Supplies

rubber gloves

cleaning spray

sponge

Spritz and wipe the mirror with vinegar or glass cleaner and a wadded up newspaper or rag. →

**Tip:** An old toothbrush is good for getting into grubby little cracks.

Maybe use a little scrubby powder or baking soda in here.

Spritz and wipe.

# CLEAN THE TOILET

**1** Put some toilet bowl cleaner or baking soda in the toilet bowl and leave it to soak while you do the rest.

**2** Spritz cleaner on the toilet tank, the top of the seat, and both the top and bottom of the lid. Wipe them off with a sponge or a rag (that you use only for the toilet).

**3** Lift up the seat, then spritz and wipe the rim of the toilet and the underside of the seat.

**4** Spritz and wipe the base of the toilet bowl and the floor around the toilet.

**5** Scrub the inside of the toilet bowl with the toilet brush, then flush.

tank

lid

seat

CLEAN ME!

rim

bowl

base

# CLEAN THE TUB AND SHOWER

**1** Pull the shower curtain out of the way.

**2** Spritz all the surfaces with cleaner, including the inside of the tub, the rim of the tub, the walls of the shower, and the faucet. Use a sponge to wipe.

**3** Use baking soda or scrubby powder on extra grubby spots.

**4** Rinse the sponge and wipe everything down.

# HOW TO PLUNGE A TOILET

It's okay! It happens! Something's not going down — so now nothing's going down. Don't panic. But also? Don't keep flushing. (Trust us on this.)

**1** Find the plunger. It looks like this.

handle

bell

UM, SO, THE TOILET? YEAH. UM...

If you can't find the plunger, you'll have to awkwardly ask somebody for one.

**2** Hold the handle of the plunger and put the bell into the toilet bowl so that it covers the drain opening. It should create a seal of air. Push down — this pushes the air out of the bell and creates a vacuum — and then pull up quickly without breaking the seal.

**3** Repeat the pushing down and pulling up on the plunger handle until whatever was stuck in the drain gets dislodged and the water goes out with a satisfying WHOOSH. Cross your fingers and flush again.

PHEW!

FLUSSHHHHHHH

# HOW TO
# MAKE A BED

**1** Stretch the fitted sheet over the mattress. Start with one corner, then do the corner diagonally opposite, then the other two. The last corner might feel really tight, like you're pulling sweatpants onto an elephant. Just tug and pull a little, and you'll get it.

**Tip:** If it's going really badly, make sure you're not putting the sheet on in the wrong direction.

**2** Lay the flat sheet over, with the top edge meeting the top edge of the mattress, and the rest hanging down evenly at the sides and bottom.

**3** Lay the blanket over the flat sheet more or less exactly.

**4** Neatly fold down the top foot or so of the blanket-sheet combo, then tuck in the bottom and sides of both like you're wrapping a present (see page 28), pulling them nice and smooth.

**5** Stuff pillows into their cases and put them where they go.

**6** Cover it all with a bedspread or duvet, if you've got one.

Don't forget to put everyone back to bed.

## How to Fold a Fitted Sheet

Just kidding. Go ahead and wad it up like a normal person.

# EDIBLE FOOD

## How to Make Meals and Find Your Way around the Kitchen

Cooking is one of our most basic life skills (hello, fire!), and it's not hard. Plus, feeding people you love is one of the best feelings on Earth.

We have to offer a couple of health-and-safety reminders about cooking, even though we know you know these things:

- Remember to wash your hands before you make food.

- Use potholders when you're working with heat, and turn off the stove or oven when you're done with it.

- Be super careful with sharp knives and appliances like blenders and food processors, and put them away safely when you're finished.

- Have fun and be creative! (Okay, that's not technically a health-and-safety reminder, but still.)

# HOW TO
# WHIP UP A SMOOTHIE

* 1 cup frozen (or fresh) fruit such as blueberries, strawberries, raspberries, blackberries, pitted cherries, or cut-up peaches, nectarines, pineapple, or mango
* 1/2 cup yogurt (any kind)
* 1 cup milk, nondairy "milk," or juice
* 1/2 of a frozen banana or 3 ice cubes
* 2 pitted dates or a drizzle of honey or maple syrup
* You might also like to add vanilla extract, shredded coconut, or grated lemon zest

Whir everything together in a blender at the highest setting until thick and smooth. (It's okay if you need to stop the blender and encourage everything a little bit with the end of a wooden spoon.)

Remember to put on the lid!

# HOW TO
# SCRAMBLE EGGS

**1** Beat together 2 eggs, a large pinch of salt, and 2 teaspoons of water in a bowl.

**2** Melt a tablespoon of butter in a pan over medium-low heat.

**3** When the melted butter seems nice and hot, pour in the eggs and scramble them, dragging a spatula across the bottom of the pan so that the egg that hasn't set (firmed up) yet can run underneath the egg that has.

**4** You might want to add some tasty things:
* grated cheese
* cream cheese
* a handful of baby spinach
* chopped herbs
* hot sauce

**5** When they seem done just right, eat them.

# HOW TO PERFECTLY BOIL AN EGG

Put an egg (or eggs) in a small pot, then cover it (them) with water by an inch or so. Put the pot on the stove, turn the heat to high, and bring the water to a boil. (You'll see big, bursting bubbles and the eggs will start moving around). Then cover the pot, turn off the burner, and let the eggs sit for exactly 10 minutes if you want the yolk firm but tender. Or try 8 minutes for a softer yolk or 12 minutes for a firmer one.

Pour the eggs and water into the sink, then run cold water over them until they're cool enough to touch. Roll each egg on the counter to crack it all over, then peel it.

Fundamental cooking skill!

Make it yummier with salt, pepper, hot sauce, or cupcake sprinkles — then eat it!

# HOW TO MAKE SALAD DRESSING

1 teaspoon salt

⅓ cup vinegar
(plain white, red wine, white wine, balsamic, apple cider, or whatever you have)

⅔ cup olive oil

Put all the ingredients in a container with a lid, screw the lid on tight, and shake it up well. Then drizzle it over a bowlful of leafy greens, and you've got salad! There will be leftover dressing. Keep it in the fridge.

## Other Possible Additions

* bloop of mustard and/or mayo (this helps keep it from separating)
* dried or fresh herbs such as oregano, basil, dill, thyme, or chives
* minced garlic or some garlic powder
* freshly ground black pepper
* other spices or seasoning blends
* grated lemon zest

# HOW TO
# MAKE A QUESADILLA

**1** Put a pan over medium-low heat and add a pat of butter or a bloop of oil.

**2** Put a tortilla in the pan and sprinkle a handful of shredded Monterey Jack or cheddar cheese over half of it.

**3** Use a spatula to fold the tortilla in half.

We call the crispy cheese at the edges "cheese crusto," and it's our favorite part.

**4** Cook until the bottom is golden-brown, then flip it with a spatula and cook until the other side is golden brown and the cheese is melted.

**5** Serve with sour cream, guacamole, and/or salsa.

# HOW TO
# MAKE YOUR FOOD
# TASTE GOOD

You made food! Yay you! Before you eat or serve it, though, taste it and make sure it's really good. If it's not, then add more seasoning.

salty

sweet

HONEY

blah buster

GARLIC POWDER

spicy

HOT SAUCE

tart

**If it's too bland,** it might need more salt. Add a pinch and taste again, then add more if it needs more. Soy sauce adds saltiness as well as a rich flavor. If the flavor goes well with whatever you made, a little soy sauce might just do the trick.

**If you still need to brighten up the flavor,** consider adding a little splash of something tart like lemon juice or vinegar.

**Is it nice and tangy,** but actually a little bit TOO tangy? Add a tiny drop of a sweetener, such as honey or maple syrup, to balance the flavor.

**Do you wish it were spicy?** Add a big grinding of black pepper, a dash of hot sauce, or a pinch of cayenne pepper.

**Is it just kind of blah?** Add a sprinkle of garlic powder or curry powder or another seasoning you love.

# HOW TO CHOP AN ONION

Don't cry, silly! It's just an onion.

**1** On a cutting board, use a large, sharp knife to trim the ends off the onion.

hand you don't write with (holding the onion)

hand you write with (holding the knife)

**2** Cut the onion in half.

**3** Peel off the papery skin.

**4** Put the onion halves flat side down on the cutting board. Cut each half into slices going from end to end. (Hold on to it so the slices stay together.) Then cut each half into slices going from side to side. You will end up with a grid of little squares.

**5** Eat. Just kidding! But lots of recipes for soups, stews, salads, and, of course, homemade onion dip start with chopping an onion. And now you know how.

Keep your onion-holding fingers curled out of the way!

# HOW TO
# ROAST A CHICKEN

**1** Heat the oven to 425°F (220°C) and put half a stick of butter on a little plate near the warm oven to soften up a little.

**2** Take the chicken out of its wrapping and reach into the front and back of it to check for a little bag of giblets (the liver, kidneys, heart, and/or neck). Throw them away, unless someone wants them.

**3** Put the chicken in a small roasting pan and sprinkle salt all over it. Lots of salt. Now rub it all over with the butter. This is kind of gross, and not very exact, and that's fine. (You can use olive oil instead if you like it better.)

**4** Put the pan in the oven and roast the chicken for 1½ hours. You want the skin to be crisp and brown. If it looks like it's going to burn at any point, turn the heat down to 400°F (200°C).

**Note:** Raw chicken is nasty and can make you sick. Wash your hands with soap and water after you touch it, *each time!* Before you grab the salt shaker, for instance.

You can stuff things inside the chicken to flavor it!
But you don't have to.

lemon
halves

rosemary
sprig

onion
halves

thyme
sprig

garlic

**5** Take it out of the oven. Poke the thigh (under the drumstick) with the tip of a sharp knife: you want the juice that comes out to look clearish rather than pink. If it's pink, then cook it a little longer, wash the knife, and test again.

**6** Let the chicken rest for 15 minutes or so, then cut it up and serve.

# HOW TO
# MAKE SPAGHETTI

**1** Fill a big pot about 2/3 full with cold water.

**2** Put it on the stove, cover it, and turn the heat to high to bring the water to a boil. When the water is boiling you'll see big, bursting bubbles.

**3** Add a handful of salt. An actual handful!

**4** Put the spaghetti (or other pasta) into the water, and use tongs or a wooden spoon to stir it around so that it doesn't all clump together.

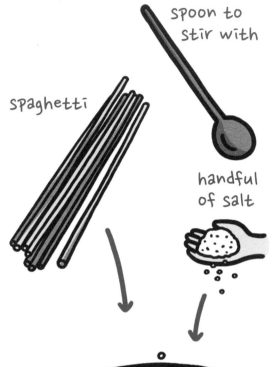

spaghetti

spoon to stir with

handful of salt

pot of boiling water

**5** Set a timer for the smallest amount of time the package recommends, put a colander in the sink, and stir the pasta some more.

**6** When the timer goes off, use tongs to fish out a piece of pasta and run it under cold water. Taste it. If it seems good, turn the heat off. If you want it cooked longer, then test it again in a minute.

**7** Use pot holders and very carefully carry the pot to the sink. Tip it away from you to pour the water and pasta into the colander. Put the pot back on the stove.

**8** Shake the colander to get the water out of the pasta. Tip the pasta back into the pot and stir in a little butter or olive oil while you think about what to do next.

**9** Eat it now! Or top it first!

**Or try:** pesto, olives, garlic powder, lemon zest, whatever you like!

grated Parmesan cheese

tomato sauce

# HOW TO SET THE TABLE

## IF THE QUEEN OF ENGLAND IS COMING

snail boat

fairy spoon

mead mug

cockle spork

fancy extra plate

rooster wrench

liverwurst knife

pumpkin carver

# IF IT'S JUST REGULAR PEOPLE

The glass goes above the knife and spoon.

The fork goes to the left of the plate.

The knife and spoon go to the right of the plate.

The folded napkin goes to the left of the fork.

Silverware goes in the order eaters will use it, from outside to inside. If there are two forks, the small salad fork goes on the outside and the big dinner fork goes on the inside. (But there will likely be only one fork.)

# POP QUIZ!

You made dinner! And everybody loved it! Yay! Afterward you:

**A**  Post a photo of the giant spaghetti-sauce mess in the kitchen. #notmyproblem

**B**  Look around at the dirty pots and pans and say, "We should probably move to a new house."

**C**  Pretend to fall asleep at the table.

**D**  Clean up after yourself and do the dishes.

**Answer:** D. But if someone says, "You cooked, so let me do the dishes," you can say, "Oh, thank you so much! I'd actually love that."

# HOW TO TURN A 33-CENT PACKAGE OF RAMEN INTO DINNER

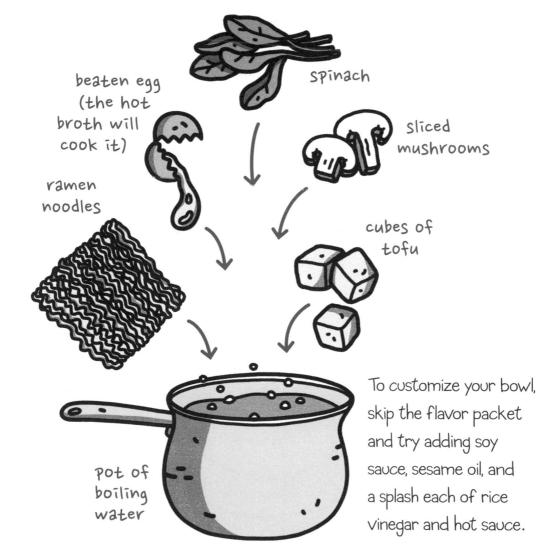

spinach

beaten egg
(the hot
broth will
cook it)

Sliced
mushrooms

ramen
noodles

cubes of
tofu

pot of
boiling
water

To customize your bowl, skip the flavor packet and try adding soy sauce, sesame oil, and a splash each of rice vinegar and hot sauce.

# YOU'RE WEARING THAT?

## How to Clean and Care for Your Clothes

Whether you're dressing for success, dressing for soccer, or dressing for just not being naked, you need to have clothes in your life. And they need to be washed, dried, put away, and even occasionally mended! Here's how.

# HOW TO
# SORT LAUNDRY

**1** Bring the laundry hamper(s) or laundry basket(s) to wherever you're going to wash the clothes.

**2** Dump the clothes onto the floor and pick out items that look like they might not go in the machine (wool sweaters, silky things, fancy things) and put them aside.

Ask an adult what to do with the things you set aside, and cross your fingers that they'll offer to deal with them.

**3** Sort the rest of the laundry into two piles: lights and darks, assuming this is your house style of doing laundry. (Some families wash all the clothes together, which is fine, too.) Traditionally, lights include undies, towels, and anything else that washes in hot water to get it really clean; darks include jeans, shirts, and other clothes that wash in warm or cold water to keep the color from bleeding out. Don't go crazy trying to determine which pile something goes in. It will be fine.

tissues

gum

gold doubloons

**4** Go through everybody's pants pockets and remove whatever you find. Finders keepers! (Not really.)

**5** Zip up zippers so they won't tear other clothes.

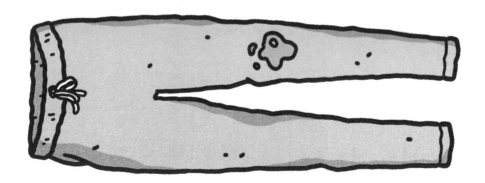

**6** Tie sweatshirt and sweatpants ties so they won't tangle or pull out.

**7** Deal with any obvious stains (see page 106).

# HOW TO
# WASH A LOAD OF LAUNDRY

## Top Loading

add soap here

## Front Loading

or maybe here

**1** Load the laundry — either in the top or in the front of the washing machine. Don't cram it too full or the clothes won't be able to move around!

**2** Add the right amount of detergent wherever it goes: into a little drawer or right into the tub of the washer. If it's liquid detergent, you can usually measure it right in its own cap. If you're supposed to add the detergent before adding the clothes, then pretend this is step 1.

**3** Turn the knob(s) to the kind of wash cycle you need or have been instructed to use. Ask an adult to teach you what the house laundry style is, then make a cheat sheet for yourself and post it near the machine. Settings you may have to select:

* how hot or cold the water is for washing and rinsing
* how fast the machine spins
* how long the cycle runs

**4** Press the "start" button.

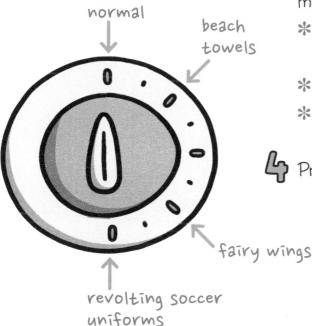

normal

beach towels

fairy wings

revolting soccer uniforms

**Fun Fact.** According to NASA, astronauts on the International Space Station don't have a lot of options for dealing with dirty clothes. One astronaut used a pair of worn underpants as a growing medium for plants, but otherwise they wear each pair of undies for 3 or 4 days and, at the end of the trip, send them off with the rest of the trash to be incinerated in outer space.

# HOW TO
# GET OUT A STAIN

Maybe you're a messy eater or your pen (or pet) leaked! Don't fret. Just deal with a stain as quickly as you can, which might mean as soon as you get home if you blooped ketchup onto yourself at the burger place, or when you're sorting laundry if you suddenly notice the grass stains on your baseball uniform.

**1** If the stain is 3-D (e.g., a dried blob of peanut butter), scrape as much of it off the fabric as you can using a plastic card (like a library or credit card) or a butter knife.

**2** If the stain is oily (e.g., bike grease or salad dressing), rub some cornstarch into it as soon as you can.

**3** Rub or spray the stain with a stain remover, checking the product's label first to make sure it's safe to use on the kind of fabric you have.

WASH ME OUT IMMEDIATELY!

**4** Leave the stain remover in until you next do laundry, unless the product says to wash it out immediately, and then use this as an excuse to pop in a load.

**5** Check your clothes when they come out of the washer, and re-treat any stains that are still visible.

**6** If a stain cannot be removed, consider sewing a decorative patch over it. Now your garment is even nicer than it was before you "ruined" it!

# HOW TO DRY A LOAD OF LAUNDRY

**1** Clean out the dryer's lint trap. There will be either a round screen that twists out or a flat screen that pulls up like a drawer at the front of the machine. Grab into the lint, swirl it off the screen, and throw it away (this is strangely satisfying). Replace the lint trap.

**2** Take your clean clothes out of the washer and put them into the dryer, shaking them out as you go to untwist clothes from each other so they won't dry in a big tangle.

Make sure you remove anything like sweaters and bras that shouldn't go in the dryer. These items should get hung or laid out to dry.

Lint trap

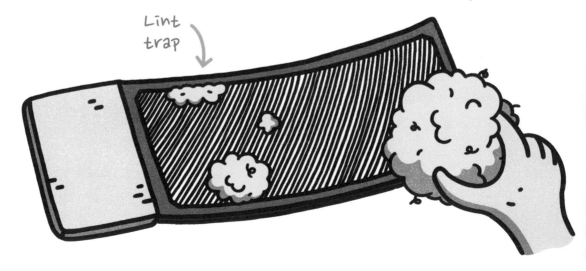

**3** Once the clothes are in the dryer, close the door and choose the proper cycle. Depending on your machine, you will probably need to choose either a preset cycle or a level of heat plus an amount of time. Ask an adult to explain this to you once, and make yourself a cheat sheet to post near the machine.

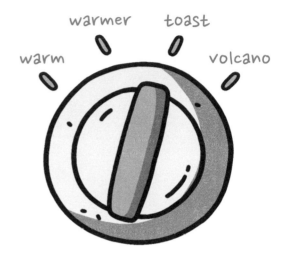

warmer   toast

warm               volcano

**4** Once the cycle is complete (this will usually take around an hour), remove the clothes as soon as you can so that they don't sit around in the dryer and get superwrinkly. Put them back in the laundry basket so you can bring them somewhere and fold them.

**5** Clean the lint trap for the next user, who will now be able to skip step 1.

# POP QUIZ!

You put your mom's favorite sweater in the dryer and now it looks like it would barely fit Eeny-Beeny, your gerbil. You:

**A** Dress Eeny-Beeny in it, and pretend not to know where it came from.

**B** Bury it in the backyard.

**C** Explain to your mother that now it can be used as felt, since shrunk wool won't unravel when you cut it. ("You're welcome!")

**D** Show it to your mom and apologize.

THAT LOOKS REALLY COZY.

**Answer:** D. But also C! The silver lining of shrunk sweaters is free crafting supplies. You can make slippers, arm warmers, or mittens out of the fabric.

# HOW TO DEAL WITH HALFWAY-DIRTY CLOTHING

Some clothes, like undies and T-shirts, go in the hamper after you wear them once. Some clothes, like sweaters and jackets, only need washing now and then.

And some clothes, like jeans and flannel shirts, can be worn more than once. We call the clothes you might wear again before washing "halfways" (halfway between dirty and clean), and they should get piled up on a chair in a disorganized way that wrinkles everything, provides a great nest for the cats, and makes you think you've lost your favorite plaid pajamas. (Not really.)

Better strategies include hanging the halfways on hooks in the closet or behind a door, or folding them and keeping them in a halfway basket next to the hamper to cue you (or someone else) to go ahead and wash your halfways if they're doing laundry anyway.

# HOW TO MANAGE CLEAN LAUNDRY

Once your laundry comes out of the dryer, you'll want to hang, fold, and/or roll your clothing so it won't look like it's been slept on by hibernating bears.

* Stack undies.
* Match socks.
* Fold pants, T-shirts, and sweatshirts.
* Put pajamas wherever they go.
* Hang dresses, shirts with buttons, and whatever else you hang.

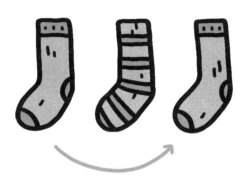

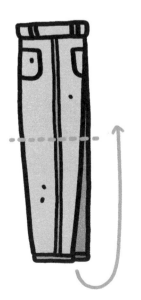

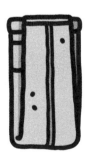

Fold pants by pairing up the legs, then folding them in half, ankle to waist (and folding them in half again, if that's what your dresser needs).

# HOW TO FOLD T-SHIRTS AND SWEATSHIRTS

**1** Lay them out flat.

**2** Fold each sleeve and side in toward the middle.

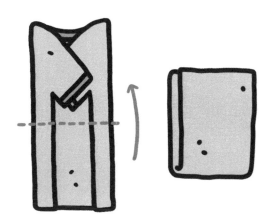

**3** Fold in half, waist to neck.

**Alternately:** roll up T-shirts and pants to keep them from creasing.

# HOW TO
# TIE A NECKTIE

Tired of your dad leaning over your shoulder to tie your tie? He is too!
This is called the Four-in-Hand Knot, and it's the easiest one we know.

**1** Drape the tie around your neck, with the wide end hanging down a foot or so below the narrow end.

**2** Cross the wide part over the narrow part.

**3** Wrap the wide part under the narrow part.

**4** Repeat steps 2 and 3, then pull the wide end up and through the loop around your neck.

*If only!*

**5** Bring the wide end down through the front of the knot.

**6** Tighten by pulling gently on the narrow end and pulling the knot up around your collar.

# HOW TO
# SEW ON A BUTTON

Whether a button fell off or you suddenly want an extra, it's really pretty easy to sew one on.

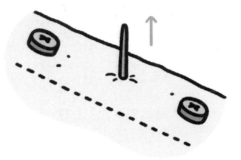

**1** Thread your needle with a foot or so of strong thread and knot one end. (See the overhand knot on page 142.) If your thread isn't especially strong, start with a longer piece, fold it in half, thread one end through the needle, and knot both ends together.

**2** Push the needle up through the fabric, back to front, in the place you want the button to end up.

**3** Thread the button onto the needle, and slide the button down the thread until it rests flat against the fabric.

**4** With the button pressed against the fabric, push the needle down through another of the button's holes and through to the underside of the fabric. Pull snug.

**5** Repeat pushing the needle up and down through the holes until you've sewn through all of the button's holes at least twice. (The button will likely have two or four holes, unless you got some kind of strange button.)

**6** Make a knot on the underside, close to the fabric. Snip the thread.

# HOW TO
# PATCH YOUR JEANS

If your jeans have deliberate holes in them, you can go ahead and wear them just the way they are! But if there are any accidental or unwanted holes, it's easy and fun to patch them up.

**1** Cut a patch from an old pair of jeans that's about an inch bigger all around than the hole you're fixing.

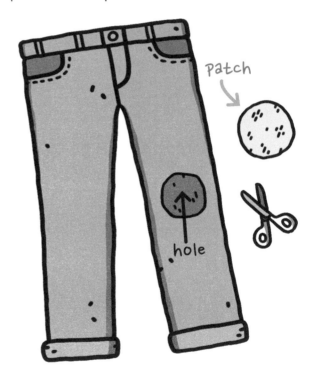

**2** With the jeans right-side out, pin the patch over the hole, making sure to pin only through one layer of your jeans, and not all the way through to the opposite side.

If you sew the leg of your jeans shut, you will be very frustrated!

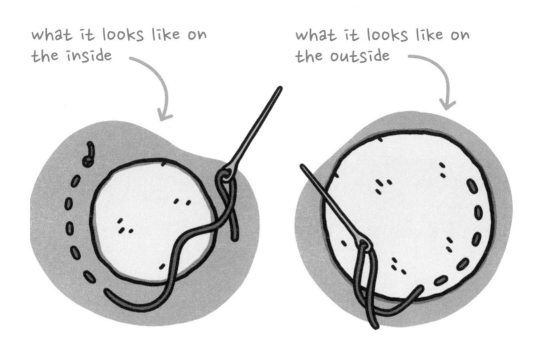

what it looks like on the inside

what it looks like on the outside

**3** Turn your jeans inside out. Thread your needle with a foot of heavy thread (embroidery thread works well for this) and knot it. Stitch around the hole through the patch, about 1/2 inch from its edge, using a running or straight stitch. (Look it up on the Internet.) Make a knot and snip the thread. Turn your jeans back right-side out.

**4** If you like, you can use a whipstitch or a buttonhole stitch to sew around the very edge of the patch and/or you can fill in the rest of the patch with decorative rows of straight stitches or little Xs.

# HOW TO
# PACK FOR A TRIP

Yay! You're going somewhere. What should you bring?

* *1 pair of underwear per day plus 1 extra for . . . good luck*

* *1 pair of socks per day*

* *1 pair of pajamas (more for longer trips), or whatever you sleep in*

* *1 shirt per day*

* 1 extra pair of pants, besides the ones you're wearing (more for longer trips)

* A sweater or sweatshirt

* Warmer, cooler, or fancier clothing if needed, plus specialty items such as a swimsuit, rain jacket, superhero cape, or sequined bow tie, as required

* Grooming items such as toothbrush, toothpaste, floss, soap, shampoo, sunscreen, etc.

* The book you're reading and a headlamp if you're likely to be sharing a room with people who go to sleep before you

* Rolling your clothes up, rather than folding them, actually makes for fewer creases once you get where you're going.

* Put extra shoes in a plastic bag before packing them.

* If you're staying at someone's house, send a thank-you note (see page 34) when you get home!

# YOUR TWO CENTS

## How to Get, Give, and Spend Money

Money doesn't actually make the world go 'round (the Earth has been spinning for 4.6 billion years, thanks to the way our solar system was formed). But you will need to earn it, save it, give it, and spend it throughout your life, and here's how.

# HOW TO MAKE MONEY

You can earn money by selling things or selling services.

**Things** will likely be stuff you've made yourself, as this is the best way to turn a profit (i.e., make more than you spend):

* lemonade or hot chocolate
* cupcakes
* popsicles
* popcorn
* jewelry
* clothing
* artwork
* your sister's rock collection (you would never)

Do a little research to find out what people in your area charge for whatever it is you're doing or selling, then get started by putting flyers in your neighbors' mailboxes. Once you get a few good customers, they'll tell their friends and you'll be a billionaire in no time! Or you'll at least make enough to support your bubble-tea habit.

**Services** means the help you have to offer, and it's most rewarding to get a job doing something you're good at:

* babysitting
* pet sitting
* dog walking
* doing yard work
* washing cars
* face painting, or performing music or magic at birthday parties and carnivals
* tutoring in a favorite school subject
* giving lessons in piano, skateboarding, knitting, or whatever you do well

* offering tech support to older people (which, if you have grandparents with smartphones, you're probably already doing for free)

**Fun Fact.** Volunteering is another great way to offer your services. Instead of money, you'll get back a tremendous sense of well-being, health, and happiness. (Volunteering is proven to release dopamine — the same brain chemical you release when you eat a chocolate bar — and boost your immune system.) Plus, you'll make the world a better place!

# HOW TO MANAGE YOUR MONEY

Yay! You made some money. Or you got some for your birthday, or because you get an allowance. Now you get to decide what to do with it. The simplest thing is to divide it into three jars:

**The Give jar** is for the money you'll give away to one or more organizations or causes or people (see page 128).

**The Save jar** is for the money you'll, um, save — either because you've got your eye on something expensive, like a phone or (thinking way ahead) a car, or because your grown-ups will expect you to contribute to your college education one day. If you save a lot, consider moving this money into a savings account (see page 130).

**The Spend jar** is for your day-to-day desires and activities: movies, treats, comic books, games (see page 132). If you have a lot of things you tend to spend money on, you can further divide your spending money into labeled envelopes: "comic books," "art supplies," "flowers for Mom" (just kidding). You've now made a budget!

# HOW TO GIVE YOUR MONEY AWAY

One of the best parts of getting money is giving some of it away. If you make charitable giving a habit now, you will probably do it your whole life, feel great about it, and make the world a better place too! Count up your "give" money at the end of the year, and decide what to do with it:

**1** **Make a list** of issues you care or worry about: global health, the environment, gender equality, endangered wildlife, disaster relief, public radio, particular political campaigns.

**2 Research organizations** that do the work you care about. There are useful websites that can tell you a lot about how an organization will use your money. Try doing an Internet search for "charity ratings."

**3 Figure out how much** money you want to give to each organization, or whether you want to give all of it to a single organization.

**4 Ask a grown-up** to help you donate, either by writing a check for you to mail or by helping you enter a credit card number online. Give your grown-up the cash in return.

**5 Feel happy.**

**Fun Fact.** Giving makes you feel good. Neuroscientists at the National Institutes of Health have used neural imaging to show that acts of generosity light up the pleasure and reward centers in your brain (the same ones that light up when you get an ice-cream cone or see your crush in the hallway).

# HOW TO SAVE MONEY

Putting money in your "save" jar is a good short-term way to keep it. But if you'll be tempted to spend it (hello, blue suede sneakers!) or if you plan to keep it for a long time, then you might want to consider other options.

**Get it out of sight.** If your main goal is to make the money harder to spend, then open an account at a local bank or credit union. You'll need an adult with you and some ID (check with the bank about what they require), and you can ask whether a savings or checking account makes more sense. Either way, you'll need to keep track of your deposits (the money you put in) and your withdrawals (the money you take out).

Money doesn't grow on trees. Sigh.

**Get interest.** If you have more than $100, look into accounts that earn interest (the amount you get back from the bank investing your money). Let's say you got an interest rate of 2 percent and you invested $100: at the end of the year, the bank would give you 2 bonus dollars.

**Make an investment.** If you have $1,000 or more and you can commit to saving it for at least a year, research other kinds of interest-earning investments, such as CDs (certificates of deposit), or even putting some money in the stock market.

* There are lots of websites that help you compare interest rates and options, including specific accounts for kids and teens.

* Wherever or however you invest, try to make sure that your money is supporting work or products you believe in. You'd hate to find out, for example, that it was getting invested in cigarettes, or working against a cause you cared about.

# HOW TO SPEND YOUR MONEY

Spending money is easy enough — but making spending decisions that have a positive impact on your life, the planet, other people, and your budget? Well, that's a little harder.

## Create less waste —

which will also cost you less money! Mend your jeans with a cool patch (see page 118); jazz up your old flip-flops with glitter glue; shop for clothes at the thrift store; check books out of the library; get a reusable cup and make your iced tea at home.

## Think about the money you spend as

your investment — in a particular company, a particular product, a particular way of treating workers or the planet. Find out more, if you need to, so you can feel confident about that investment.

Watch the short animated film "The Story of Stuff" to understand more about the cycles of mass production and waste in our culture.

**Leave the store** if you're suddenly dying to buy something you know you don't need and haven't even thought about before (we call this "an attack of the wanties"). Then see if the wanties go away.

**Keep in mind (and sight)** the big item you're saving for — a horse, a bike, college, a phone, concert tickets, a trip to visit your best friend from camp — by taping a photo of it to your wallet. Then when you go to spend your money, you'll remember why you might want to save it instead.

**Consider the research** that shows that spending money on experiences — trips, concerts, meals, time with friends — brings more pleasure than spending money on things.

The experience of shopping is kind of a confusing middle ground! We sometimes jokingly call stores "thing museums" to put us in a looking-rather-than-shopping mind-set.

# POP QUIZ!

## What's a good reason to buy something you don't actually need?

**A** According to the ad, having/wearing/drinking it will make you beautiful, wealthy, and popular.

**B** According to gender stereotypes, you need to have/wear/drink it to be the "right" kind of boy/girl/man/woman.

**C** If you don't have/wear/drink it, you will look like Shrek and also have zero friends.

**D** Having/wearing/drinking it would make you happy.

**Answer:** D. You're too smart for marketing campaigns that assume you can't use your brain, need to conform, or only care about what other people think. (Too bad they already spent all their money on those ads! Ha ha ha!)

# HOW TO
# HAVE A DEBIT CARD

A debit card lets you buy something without using real-life cash. But it's different from a credit card because you're only spending your own money. (With a credit card, you're borrowing money until you pay your bill.) A debit card makes it impossible to spend more money than you actually have — which means you won't ever owe money, and you won't ever pay interest.

There are two main kinds of debit cards:

* One is connected to your bank account, so anything you spend is subtracted from the amount of money you've deposited in your account.

* The other is prepaid, which is kind of like a gift card: you (or your grandparents or favorite aunt) load money onto the card, and then anything you spend is subtracted from that amount.

**1** When it comes time to pay for the book, movie ticket, or chai you want to buy, slide your debit card through (or insert it into) the card reader at the register.

**2** Then you punch in a security code, called a PIN (or personal identification number), which tells the bank it's really you (you'll choose or be assigned this number with the card).

THANK YOU!

**Fun Fact.** The personal identification number "1234" accounts for more than 10 percent of all PINs. Maybe pick something different?

**3** Look up from all the sliding and punching to thank the person who checked you out.

# HOW TO
# CALCULATE THE TIP

If someone serves you kimchi tacos at a restaurant or delivers a pesto pizza to your home or drives the taxi you're taking to a Broadway play (#dreaming), then you will pay them a tip. This is an extra amount beyond the cost of the service or purchase, and it's not really optional because folks in service jobs count on this money to make a living wage.

**As a general rule,** tip 20 percent of the total cost of the bill or charge. An easy trick for this is to calculate 10 percent, and then double it.

$5.00 = total cost of bill

Figuring out 10 percent is easy: it usually just means lopping off the last zero. If your kimchi tacos were $5.00, then you would calculate 10 percent as 50¢, and then double it: $1.00. (If your bill was $4.90, you could just round up to $5.00 first.)

10% = 1/10 = $.50 or 50¢

$.50 × 2 = $1.00

$1.00 = 20% tip

**An exception is pizza delivery,** where you can tip less — 10 or 15 percent — but you should tip at least $5 per delivery, even if that's more than 15 percent of the cost of the pizza.

**If you see a tip jar at a café** where you're ordering at the counter, you can put $1 or some change in it, especially if you're planning to hang out for a long time talking to your friends over a single mug of chai.

minimum tip for delivery

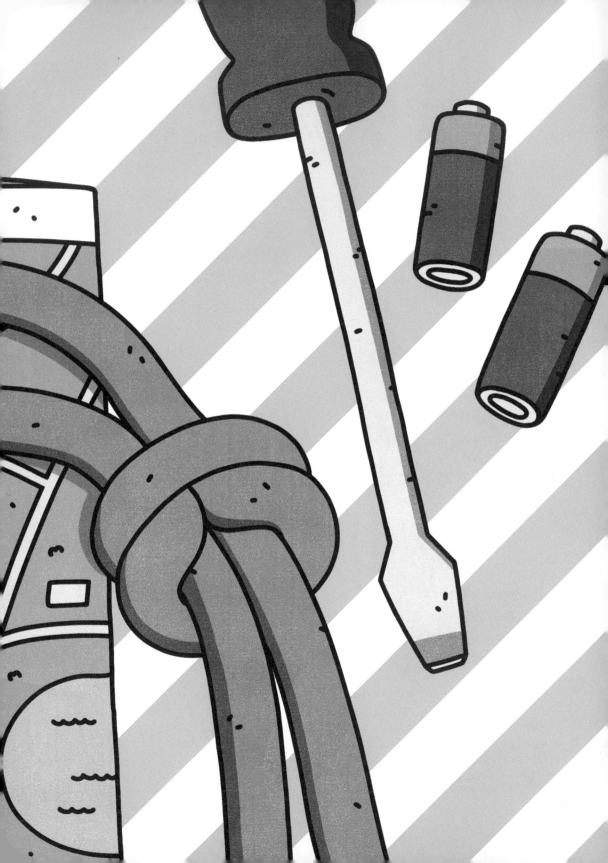

# USEFUL SKILLS

## How to Do Basic Important Things

- - - - - - - - - - - - - - - - - -

There are some things you will just need to know how to do on and off throughout your life. We've gathered up a few of them here to make a chapter that's kind of a collage of repair and improvisation.

# HOW TO
# TIE BASIC KNOTS

Knots tend to solve attachment problems, like "How do you attach two ropes together?" or "How do you attach one thing to another thing?" And knowing how to tie a couple of knots is especially helpful if you're going to be sailing, camping, rock climbing, or mountaineering.

## OVERHAND KNOT

An overhand knot makes a kind of stopper at the bottom of your rope, string, or thread, and it's the basis for lots of other knots. It's also useful on its own to keep a rope from unraveling or to keep the beads from falling off the bottom of your string.

Make a loop of rope and pass the end through.

Pull to tighten.

## SQUARE KNOT

A square knot is a strong, attractive way to tie together two ends of rope, to attach two ropes together, or to secure one rope around something else. It's an important knot for sailors and scouts, but you can also use it in crafts such as macramé.

Hold an end of the rope in each hand. Pass the working end (the gray one) over and under the standing end (the green one).

Pass the working end (still the gray one) over the standing (green) end.

Pass the working end under and up through the standing end. Tighten by pulling both ends at the same time.

# CLOVE HITCH

Used by boaters and climbers, this is a great knot for tying a rope to a pole or a line to a mast.

Pass the working end of the rope around the pole (or rod or tree limb).

Continue wrapping over the standing end and around the pole a second time.

Thread the end under itself and pull tight.

# BRAID

Okay, this isn't really a knot, but it's a fun and useful skill to know.

Start with three lengths of rope or yarn or hair or whatever you want to braid, and bind the ends together with tape or a rubber band. (In the case of hair, someone's scalp will do this for you.)

Pass one outside strand across the center strand.

Then pass the other outside strand across the new center strand.

Repeat, alternating one side and then the other, until you come to the ends, which you can knot (unless it's hair — then use a hair band please).

# HOW TO BUILD A FIRE

Outdoor fire pit, woodstove, or fireplace — wherever you build it, most of the fire-making principles are the same.

You need a bucket of water to put out an outdoor fire.

Place tinder in the center of the fire.

Arrange kindling around and on top of the tinder.

Lean larger pieces of firewood against the cone of kindling.

**1** First, if you're outside, make sure there's not a ban or restriction on campfires, and that you're using a designated fire pit. Be sure you have a bucket of water to put the fire out when you're done with it. If you're inside, make sure you know where the fire extinguisher is.

**2** Gather the tinder. This is the easily lit dry material that will be at the center of your fire: twisted-up newspaper, shredded bark, dry pine needles, and, in a pinch (if you didn't eat them all), tortilla chips. Pile this up in the center of your fire area.

**3** Arrange the kindling — twigs and small sticks — around and on top of the tinder, in an upside-down ice-cream cone shape. Don't pack it too tight, since your fire will need air to breathe. Hold some kindling back to feed the fire as it gets going.

**4** Lean larger pieces of firewood against the cone of kindling you've built, balancing them against each other like a game of Jenga you're planning to win. Hang on to your biggest logs for now.

**5** Use a match or lighter to ignite the tinder. If the kindling doesn't seem inclined to catch, you can gently blow on the fire or fan it with a piece of cardboard or a flattened cereal box.

**6** Feed the fire some of your reserved kindling as necessary until it seems nice and raging. You can add your biggest logs once you're sure that the larger pieces have caught.

**7** Make s'mores/sing songs/tell ghost stories.

**8** When you're done (if you're outside), dump water on the fire until the flames go out, then stir the fire with a stick while you dump more water on it until the site is cool. If you're inside, make sure the fire is safely contained in the fireplace or woodstove before you leave the room.

# HOW TO
# CHANGE BATTERIES

Your headlamp, wristwatch, graphing calculator, or smoke detector died. Sad! But you can revive it with new batteries.

**1 First, figure out where the batteries are.** They're usually in a special compartment that has a little snap-open door, except in flashlights, where the batteries tend to live behind a screwed-on cap.

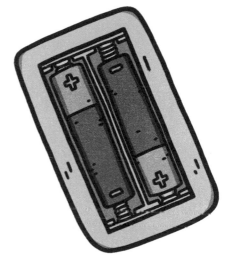

**2 Before you take the old batteries out,** study how they're arranged so you'll know how to put in the new batteries. If it's a single little button battery, figure out which side is up and which is down. If there are multiple batteries, they might be arranged in alternating directions, like a group of cousins sleeping head-to-toe in a bed. The + end of the battery will push up against a little plate, and the − end of the battery will push into a coily spring. (A 9-volt battery will have a snap connection instead.)

**3** **Remove the batteries,** figure out what kind/size they are, and make sure you have the right number of new (or charged) batteries.

**4** **Put in the new batteries,** and make sure they're all the same: don't mix old and new batteries, or rechargeable and disposable batteries.

**5** Snap the little door closed.

## A FEW BATTERY SIZES

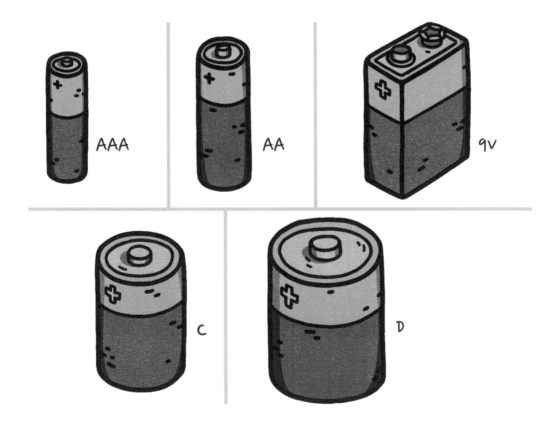

AAA

AA

9V

C

D

# POP QUIZ!

You replaced the batteries in your headlamp because the light was very dim. The old batteries still work a little, though. Now what?

**A** Pin a gold star to yourself.

**B** Mix them back in the package with the new batteries, since someone else will probably be overjoyed when their calculator conks out halfway through the SATs.

**C** Leave them on the coffee table, kitchen counter, or dining table. It seems crazy to throw out perfect barely working batteries!

**D** Recharge the batteries if they're rechargeable, or, if they're disposable, put them in the trash (unless the package tells you to recycle them or to dispose of them in a special way).

**Answer:** D. (Then, if you want, A.)

# HOW TO TIGHTEN A SCREW

If something is loose — the faucet, a chair, your bookshelf – fixing it might be as simple as tightening a screw! To make sure you pick the right tool for the job, look at the screw first.

If it's a flat-head screw, it will have a straight line across it.

If it's a Phillips-head screw, it will have an X.

Find the screwdriver that matches your screw: a flat-head screwdriver will have a flat tip; a Phillips-head screwdriver will have a pointy tip in the shape of a cross.

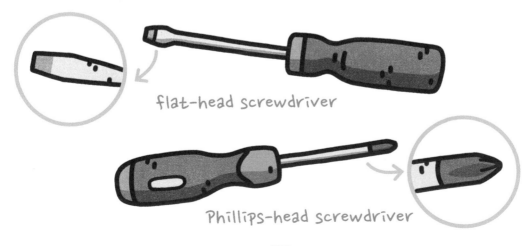

flat-head screwdriver

Phillips-head screwdriver

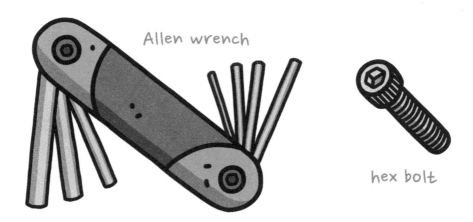

Allen wrench

hex bolt

Once you figure out the type and size of screwdriver you need, stick the tip into the slot or X of your screw and turn the screwdriver toward the right to tighten it.

"Righty Tighty/Lefty Loosey" is a good mnemonic device to remember which way to turn the screwdriver — and you can use it for light bulbs too.

righty tighty

lefty loosey

When something on your bike, skates, or skateboard needs tightening, you might need a different tool. If instead of a straight line or an X you see a little hexagonal shape in the middle of your screw or bolt, then you need an Allen wrench (or hex key). An Allen wrench is usually an L-shaped metal bar with a hexagonal head at each end. (It might also come as part of a set in a Swiss Army knife-type of body or there might be a bunch of them connected by a ring.) You'll need to find the right size wrench before tightening or loosening your screws or bolts.

# HOW TO USE A SWISS ARMY KNIFE

Whether you're an outdoorsy fish-scaling kind of person or more of a living-room whittler, a Swiss Army knife is so useful and cool. No matter what tools you have on yours, here are some all-purpose tips for keeping yourself (and everyone around you) safe while you use it.

cat head — corkscrew — punch — key ring — toothpick and/or tweezers — large blade — can opener — smaller flat-head screwdriver — saw — small blade — bottle opener — bigger flat-head screwdriver

The large blade is useful for whittling (always push the sharp edge away from you).

The punch is good for carving out holes in wood or leather.

Try opening a can of beans to practice using the can opener.

✳ Use only one blade or tool at a time.

✳ To open a blade or tool, hold the body of the knife in your nonwriting hand. Stick the thumbnail of your other hand in the little groove and carefully pull it out from the body of the knife until it's open enough for you to safely grasp it, then open it the rest of the way.

✳ Never grab the sharp side of a blade.

✳ Cut, punch, or carve away from your body so you'll be safe if the knife slips.

✳ When you're done, make sure the blade or tool is clean (rubbing alcohol on a cotton ball will remove sap), then pop it back into the body of the knife. Do this safely by holding the sides of the knife's body with one hand, keeping all your fingers away from the slot that the tool or blade is going back into, and then using your other thumb to push on the dull side of the blade toward the body of the knife until it snaps into place.

**Fun Fact.** The Wenger Giant is the biggest Swiss Army knife in the world, and it has 87 tools!

# HOW TO
# READ A ROAD MAP

Reading a paper map is a great skill to have not only because you could lose your GPS signal sometime, but also because it helps you understand where you are in the world. Plot your route before walking, riding your bike, or navigating while someone's driving (or while you're driving yourself, yoiks).

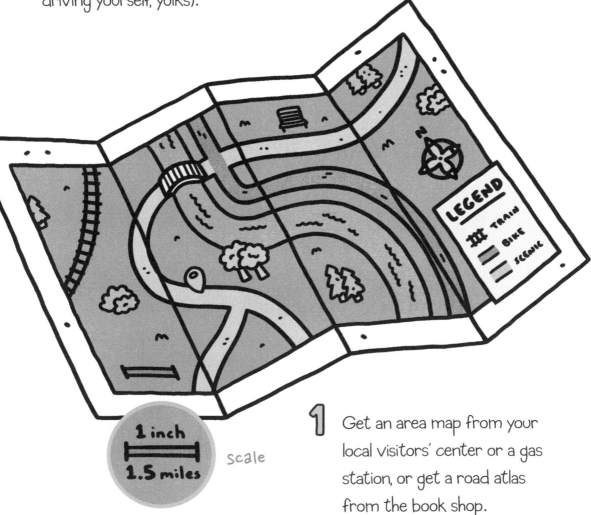

**LEGEND**
TRAIN
BIKE
SCENIC

1 inch
1.5 miles
scale

1 Get an area map from your local visitors' center or a gas station, or get a road atlas from the book shop.

**2** **Learn the legend.** The map will have a box somewhere that translates its symbols.

**3** **Understand the map's scale.** This will translate distance on the map into distance in real life.

**4** **Find yourself.** This is like the "start" arrow on a maze — also called "point A." If you're not sure where you are, see if you can find the nearest roads or landmarks.

**5** **Figure out where you're going** — the end point, also called "point B." Plot your route. Consider whether it will be scenic, if you'll travel on small roads or big highways, or, if you're riding your bike, what the best bike routes are.

**6** **If you get lost** ("point Z") just call this a "learning detour." Consult your map and start over.

If you're hiking you might use a topographic map, which gives you a 3-D sense of the land. Concentric contour lines show elevation: the closer together the lines, the steeper the uphill or downhill. You can tell the difference between uphill or downhill by the number next to the line. The number represents the elevation in feet: increasing numbers show an uphill, and decreasing numbers show a downhill.

# HOW TO BE HAPPY

You won't experience happiness every second of your life — and you don't need to. But you can definitely maximize your feelings of joy, peace, connectedness, and purpose.

## Make healthy habits

for yourself that include eating nourishing food and getting the amount of sleep you need (or as close to it as you can). Less root beer! More kale!

## Spend time outside

and in nature. Consider walking or riding your bike instead of getting a ride. Take a stroll after dinner, with a headlamp on if it's dark out. Look up at the sky!

## Spend time every day feeling grateful

for the people you love, your pets, your home, the hundreds of ways you're lucky, even if you don't always feel like it. Gratitude increases your feel-good brain chemicals.

**Be generous** with your time, your money, and your care. Give more and it will come back to you in happiness and, if you ever need it, in someone giving back to you.

**Do real stuff with your hands.** Neuroscientists have shown that doing meaningful physical activities — knitting, chopping wood, making food, anything with a tangible, useful outcome — releases natural antidepressants that increase your sense of well-being.

**Relatedly, spend less time on your phone** in general and social media in particular, since these activities can actually reduce your sense of well-being.

**Don't dwell on mishaps or mistakes.** Do whatever you need to do next — apologize, solve a problem, or learn what went wrong — then forgive yourself and move on. This is how we grow.

**Fight injustice.** Stick up for lonely or bullied kids at your school. Fight discrimination. Advocate for people in need. Call your political representatives. March. Donate money. Know what you believe and why.

**Smile more!** Unless you don't feel like smiling. And then don't.

# THANK YOU

Oh, thank you, thank you! To my friends and family, for being everything to me, but especially my kids: Birdy Newman, whose stubborn hatred of being *explained to* is what prompted me to write this book in the first place, and Ben Newman, who — along with Birdy — patiently, intelligently, and hilariously read and improved early drafts. Their dad, Michael, makes our lives happy, fun, and easy, and I adore him. My wise, funny friend Ron Lieber generously bettered the money chapter.

Debbie Fong's dreamboat illustrations made me understand the book I was hoping to make, because it's this. Thank you, Debbie!

Everyone at Storey is both crazily talented and wildly encouraging: Deborah Balmuth and Deanna Cook championed this idea at every stage with their usual enthusiasm and flair; Michal Lumsden edited the book with grace, good humor, and a kind eye; Alee Moncy always brims with ideas for making the most of everybody's gifts; Alethea Morrison is a brilliant, intuitive art director; and Mars Vilaubi cheerfully and expertly took photos and made videos.

And you, dear reader! Thank you for holding this book in your hands, and for wanting to know how to do more stuff and be your best self. That's how we'll change the world.